The Way to Life

The Way to Life

Fr Bishoy Kamel

ST SHENOUDA PRESS
SYDNEY, AUSTRALIA
2025

The Way To Life
Fr Bishoy Kamel

Translated by: Michael Rizkalla

COPYRIGHT © 2025
St Shenouda Press

All rights reserved. Except for brief quotations in critical publications or reviews, no part of this book may be reproduced in any manner without prior written permission from the publisher.

ST SHENOUDA PRESS
8419 Putty Rd,
Putty, NSW, 2330
Australia

www.stshenoudapress.com

ISBN 13: 978-1-7638415-5-0

All scripture quotations, unless otherwise indicated, are taken from the New King James Version®. Copyright © 1982 by Thomas Nelson, Inc. Used by permission. All rights reserved.

Table of Conten

Preface to the first edition

Preface to the second edition

CHAPTER ONE   1

The beginning of the Way - The Need

CHAPTER TWO   17

Freedom in the Way

CHAPTER THREE   29

Sacred Love in The Way

CHAPTER FOUR   55

I Am the Way

The beginning of the Way… An absolute need for the work of the Holy Spirit.

The middle of the Way… A sacred love, leading to peace and joy

The end of the Way… A complete union with the Lord Jesus Christ

For He is
The Way, The Truth, and The Life

Preface to the first edition

Whoever desires to become my disciple, let him deny himself, and take up his cross, and follow Me.

The Lord Jesus came to establish a Way to eternal life for us so that we can follow His footsteps. None of His followers expected the Way to be so difficult. Perhaps some disciples protested, saying that if the Way was easy like other religions, it would have attracted more followers to Jesus. Some followers even left Jesus due to His teachings saying "This is a hard saying; who can understand it?" (John 6:60).

Most importantly, Jesus is insistent that all His commandments be followed, as they are the Way for us to become children of God.

Recalling the sermon on the mountain, we will find His commandments very difficult… whoever slaps you on your right cheek turn the other to him, also…love your enemies, bless those who curse you, do good to those who hate you, and pray for those who spitefully use you and persecute you, **that you may be sons of your Father in heaven.** (Matthew 5).

So either we believe and obey these commandments or we will be rejected by Heaven, even if we were known on earth as Christians!

Christ reveals to us that sin is not accounted to us only at the level of action, but begins as a sin of thought eg. whoever looks at a woman to lust for her has already committed adultery with her in his heart, and Jesus said as a consequence, the whole body will be cast into hell. (Matthew 5:28-30).

Jesus confirms at the end of the sermon that the Way is difficult and narrow "Enter by the narrow gate; for wide *is* the gate and broad *is* the Way that leads to destruction, and there are many who go in by it… "Because narrow *is* the gate and difficult *is* the Way which leads to life" (Matthew 7:13,14)

Let us then ask ourselves: Are we on the right Way? And if we are not, then what profit is it to us if we gain the whole world, and lose our own souls?

Nevertheless, I want to emphasise that even though the Way is difficult, its yoke is easy and its burden is light, even delightful, and is within the capability of the weakest person. Due to the fact that Jesus came to save everyone who believes in Him, He set a Way easily followed even by the least knowledgeable and understanding.

At the beginning of the Way, it is difficult to disengage

from the entanglements of this world; which we are not part of. Yet after a little time struggling in the Way, Christ becomes our victory, a testimony of His mighty power working in our weakness, a total peace even when we are faced with martyrdom.

Eventually, the end of the Way is a complete union with God to become partners in the Divine nature and heirs with Jesus.

The beginning of the Way is the believer's recognition of the need for the Holy Spirit to work in his life and to unite him with a stronger nature than hid weak one.

It's an acknowledgement of our weakness and a plea to God's strength which transforms us from weak to strong people.

It transforms us from "O wretched man that I am! Who will deliver me from this body of death?" to "I can do all things through Christ who strengthens me".

It is a test of the strength of our faith.

Yet, the middle of the road is a sacred love leading to complete peace, victory, joy and growth.

Let us examine someone loving God and living in peace, will it be hard for him to keep God's difficult commandments? If someone loves God, the fountain of Love, then, he will without a doubt love his friends, relatives, colleagues and even his enemies.

Conversely, whoever finds God's commandments heavy is the one with an indifferent relationship with God. Hence, when you fail to listen to God's commandments then you are not at peace with God. You are then acting with your failing human nature and the outcome is a complete failure.

Examine your relationship with God first before your relationship with others.

The end of the Way is the complete union with Christ, and more than that, you will experience what is deeper: that Christ Himself is the only Way, otherwise His coming wouldn't be necessary.

How astonishing it is when Thomas didn't know the Way and said to Jesus how do we go to the Father, we do not know the Way?! Jesus replied in deep sorrow "I am the Way, the truth, and the life."

Still, a sinful woman poured the fragrant oil over Jesus so He loved her and forgave her many sins because she loved much.

Moreover, the tax collector who made it through the Way of needing Jesus, consequently, went down to his house justified after his prayer.

Preface

And what could be said with regards to the right hand thief who knew the Way when the disciple didn't?!

Accordingly, I want you to be meticulous about your life, my friend, even if you were a disciple to Jesus, a great servant or a novice; Are you in the Way?

It's crucial to follow the footsteps of those who made it to the end of the Way. This is more guaranteed than choosing for ourselves unsecured 'ways'.

Therefore, when we come across characters who one day met Christ and conversed with Him, we have to put ourselves in their places, awaiting the Lord's words to them as if they were to us.

St Mary's Church at Moharam Bek,

Sunday School- Youth meeting year 1959

Preface to the second edition

There are a plenty of books all over the world, but there only one called "The Book", and this is the "Holy Bible".

Likewise, everyone has a 'way' in life and numerous are the 'ways' in the world, yet there is one Way, well known, that when the definite article is added it becomes "The Way" leading to eternal life.

This is Jesus who said referring to Himself "I am the Way, the truth and the life".

It's amazing how Jesus is the life as well as the "Way" leading to the life; this is true because without Jesus, no one can reach the Father or the eternal life.

And since the book in hand is "The Way to Life", this makes it an old yet new book due to its invariable topic, as Jesus is yesterday, today and forever.

Hence, we issue the second edition, providing an opportunity for youth who haven't read this book, as the first edition ran out of print over ten years ago.

It's a book worth reading for every youth, and every

believer who is truthful in their faith and their will to proceed in the Way to eternal life.

It uncovers a lot of deviations we make, perhaps unwillingly or unknowingly leading to divergence from "the Way". Then we spend our whole lives in struggle, serving and using the multiple means of grace provided to us by the Holy Church, yet, lacking significant progress in "the Way".

My beloved brethren, let us read this book which is small in size yet great in practical utility, with a spirit of contemplation and quiet prayer, so God may bless our reading and you may get the desired benefit, walking with steady steps looking unto the author and finisher of our faith, the Lord Jesus.

We ask this for you through the intercessions of our mother the virgin St Mary, the prayers of our fathers, the pure saints, and the supplications of our blessed and honourable father, His Holliness Pope Kyrillos the sixth, may God prolong his life.

St Mary's Church at Moharam Bek,

Sunday School- Toba 1686 January 1970

CHAPTER ONE
The beginning of the Way- The Need

Two men went up into the temple to pray; the one a Pharisee, and the other a tax collector. The Pharisee stood and prayed thus with himself, 'God, I thank You that I am not like other men—extortioners, unjust, adulterers, or even as this tax collector. I fast twice a week; I give tithes of all that I possess.' And the tax collector, standing afar off, would not so much as raise his eyes to heaven, but beat his breast, saying, 'God, be merciful to me a sinner!' I tell you, this man went down to his house justified rather than the other; for everyone who exalts himself will be humbled, and he who humbles himself will be exalted. (Luke 18:11-14).

If we give the chance to a group of people to judge this situation, they would say that the Pharisee was much more righteous than the tax collector; or at the least, the Pharisee is less sinful than the tax collector. But, the Lord sees that the tax collector was much more righteous than the Pharisee, because he is a humble man, who admitted his own failures.

And if we ponder the feeling of need, we find it a dual experience; firstly, the experience of humility and secondly, the experience of faith.

The experience of humility;

Every one of us aims to do good, even that tax collector. But, we all have experienced our powerlessness in doing good. Yet not the Pharisee, why didn't he feel the powerlessness and humility?

This is because he, looking outwardly, judged others saying "I am not like other men" but the tax collector focused inwardly and as a consequence, he could not look up to God, because when he pondered the sin that is inhabitant within him, he found it exceedingly terrible, so he poured out his soul before the Lord while fighting against his sin and acknowledging his weakness…

First, how do we discover our sins and our weak nature?

1. By quiet meditation;

Socrates taught us the following principle as a starting point of the way to wisdom: "Know yourself". The man who is very busy with lesser things which represent the concerns of the world, unfortunately, does not save for himself any quiet time to meditate on what he has accomplished throughout his day or stand before God in prayer while repenting of his sins.

How many times have I committed sins against God? How many times did I do good things? Do you not know that he who lives in sin, is destined to repeat what was done by Judas the traitor and the Jewish leadership who insulted, rejected and despised Christ?

How did St. Augustine explore his own sins and how did he write his confessions? By pondering his past life. And if we think about Paul's analysis of his feelings regarding this experience, …

'For I know that in me (that is, in my flesh) nothing good dwells; for to will is present with me, but how to perform what is good I do not find (Roman 7:18).

O wretched man that I am! who shall deliver me from this body of death? (Romans 7:24)

So, the time of solitude is necessary to explore and reveal the inside of ourselves, and it is enough that "our sins against God" be the core of this contemplative time rather than the irrelevant details of who did what to whom.

On the other hand, those who overly concern themselves in this world and focus only on their physical appearance and on how they present before others, find it too difficult to sit alone and delve into their own shortcomings.

Let us go back to the Old Testament to discover what sin is, what are its effects and what was the necessary cleansing procedure for salvation.

The sinner would admit his sin before a priest and be cleansed from it; presenting a sin and transgression offering. On this altar of the burnt offering, the fire was perpetual as a witness of the eternal horror of sin.

But despite all of this, Paul the Apostle, in his letter to the Hebrews, says "For it is not possible that the blood of bulls and of goats should take away sins" (Hebrews 10:4) for this, Christ came and offered himself as a sin offering. "And without shedding of blood there is no remission of sin" (Hebrews 9:22).

So then, sin at any level is an assault upon God's righteousness and at the same time it is an offence against the human soul who is originally created by God "in His image". This image was united with Christ and became one with Him.

St Paul asks 'Shall I then take the members of Christ and make them members of a harlot? Certainly not!' (1Corinthians 6:15) so, do you know now why Christ is suffering when we commit sin? Because, we are a part of Him "we have been united with Him" He died and resurrected, so that all those who believe in Him should live no longer for themselves, but for him who died for them, and rose again.

That's why the prophet David says, "Against You, You only, have I sinned, And done this evil in Your sight" (Psalm 51:4). So sin, even if it is committed in secret, away from human eyes, is still committed against God.

It is this fact that enabled Joseph, the righteous, to consider the sin that his master's wife demanded was actually a sin against God Himself: "how then can I do this great wickedness, and sin against God?" (Genesis 39:9).

And when I stand before God in prayer, where did I get that right? David himself prays "Lord, who may abide in Your tabernacle? Who may dwell in Your holy hill? He who walks uprightly, And works righteousness, And speaks the truth in his heart;" (Psalm 15:1).

If "the heavens are not clean in his sight." "and his angels he charged with folly" so, who am I to stand before Him? The answer; only through the tax collector's approach! That is to beat upon my chest, humbling myself and saying, 'God be merciful to me a sinner'.

Paul the Apostle was aware of what he had done before coming to God and reminds his disciple Timothy in his epistle, «I am the chief of sinners"; he comprehends the extent of his human weakness and he realises that sin is so ingrained in his flesh, that he is the chief among sinners.

2. Quiet meditation leads to the release of the spirit.

Having a calm, contented body and soul sets the scene for the soul to desire reunification with its creator, Jesus Christ. The natural existence of the soul is to be with God and when man fell into sin, he sank into the world of sin, but his soul still longs for God.

This explains the deep feeling within us that drives us to seek God, and this is the secret of our love toward Him, even when it is not acted upon.

The soul's liberation is the result of the quietness of thoughts, senses and freedom from worldly cares, riches and pleasures.

This marvellous thing, you may have experienced during the quiet moments in your life, as in quiet retreat for example. You have also doubtlessly realised that when you are occupied with the world and its riches, you can't have this simple, spiritual conversation with God. You may have complained many times that you are not able to pray to God. Do you realise the reason now? It is because you lack quietness of the soul.

3. During meditation & quietness, your soul will be liberated, and you will realise your sins, then you will experience Jesus Christ.

You will realise that Jesus is able to justify the ungodly,

and that He did not come for righteous people but for sinners; based on that, He granted salvation to the tax collector.

During your retreat, it is sufficient that you meditate on the Cross of the Lord of glory. Upon this Cross, He destroyed the sting of death, which is sin, and on this Cross, He laid the iniquity of us all, so we have risen with Him free of sins. On this Cross, He revealed His love toward us, in that, while we were yet sinners, Christ died for us. Moreover, His love is manifested on the Cross, as he laid down Himself for the sinners. We then realize how horrible the sin is that crucified Jesus.

Finally, conclude your quiet session with a feeling of grateful and complete humility.

1. The sin we do is an offence against Jesus Himself.
2. Every offence stems from the corruption of our nature.
3. Every good deed is from God, as He is good in His nature.

Application:

Consider examining yourself quietly for sometime, pondering firstly only your sins, and then on Jesus' cross, and write down what God reveals to you during your meditation.

Second: Striving against sin

Ask yourself these questions; Don't I take the Lord's body and blood? Aren't I the temple of the Holy Spirit, who dwells in me? Why then do I return to my sin?

The answer to this question is very simple. God gave us all these capabilities, but He will not impose our salvation on us; He is standing and knocking at the door. If we open, He will come in and dine. The first step – opening the door - is hence our duty, and afterwards He will come in, dine and do wonders in our lives; victory, love, joy and peace.

The first step is the fruit of our striving, which is the beginning of the Way. Indeed, we cannot conquer alone, but God won't work in our lives if we refuse His help or don't seek Him.

"Fight with me in prayers", was the petition that Paul requested several times in his service, because he saw God as the source of all generosity, yet the pre-requisite for God's generosity is striving in prayers. Contemplate on the parable of the unjust judge, when he stood and avenged the woman for her persistence. Let us strive in our prayers, and strive to bloodshed against sins and the world's pleasures, and strive to control our thoughts and our senses, so that we don't allow anything that doesn't match the holiness of our souls to enter our minds through them. Let us strive to be filled by the Holy Spirit so He can work in our life, and support our weakness and turn our failure to success, our weakness to strength and our defeat to victory.

The Holy Spirit dwelling within us won't bestow upon us His blessings and strengt except by prayer and persistence.

The victory in our life is the fruit of our striving supported by the strength of the Holy Spirit.

Here we should always remember that we won't win just by our striving, regardless of our strength or will. We need to remember that the Holy Spirit can't impose His strength upon us.

Which striving do we mean? The striving during prayers, the very same struggle that Jacob had with God and was then blessed by Him. It is this same struggle and striving which the saints pursued in their prayers through sweat, tears, kneeling and fasting. That's how God's kingdom is 'taken by force', and the life of glory and union with God is the reward of striving in prayers.

The Christian struggle is also the striving against the covetousness of the world. It is the seeking of abstinence from the world's pleasures, that is why the Bible counted Lot's striving against sin as righteousness; "and delivered righteous Lot, who was oppressed by the filthy conduct of the wicked, for that righteous man, dwelling among them, tormented his righteous soul from day to day by seeing and hearing their lawless deeds" (2Peter2 :7-8).

When Lot lived among the wicked, he kept his hearing, his sight and his soul away from sin by painful striving to keep such thoughts from entering his mind, and that's why he was considered righteous. So too was Joseph in his resistance to Potiphar's wife, which was a strong reason for why God poured spiritual blessings on him later on in his story.

Application:

Being filled with the Holy Spirit is the experience gained from striving in prayers, so treat any problem, especially a spiritual one, by praying strongly about it and using kneeling prostrations during your prayers (Metania), that God might resolve it for you.

The testing of Faith:

The Bible tells the stories of many men of faith, in the Old and New Testaments. Faith in God and His word was a testing of these men of God, and when they grew in their faith, they became sons of God ... So, what is this testing of faith? It is simply a number of faith related questions. As follows:

The beginning of the Way- The Need

- Do you believe that only God can rise from the dead?

- Do you believe that only God can create life from death?

This was the testing of our fathers:

"By faith Abraham, when he was tested, offered up Isaac, and he who had received the promises offered up his only begotten son, of whom it was said, In Isaac your seed shall be called, concluding that God was able to raise him up, even from the dead..." (Hebrews 11:17-19)

How could God promise Abraham nations through Isaac and his seed in the future, but on ask Abraham to sacrifice his son?

But Abraham knew that only God was able to raise Isaac from the dead, and Saint Paul the apostle wrote about him "in the presence of Him whom he believed—God, who gives life to the dead and calls those things which do not exist as though they did" (Romans 4:17).

St Paul passed this same faith-test in Asia and revealed it, writing "For we do not want you to be ignorant, brethren, of our trouble which came to us in Asia: that we were burdened beyond measure, above strength, so that we despaired even of life. Yes, we had the sentence of death in ourselves that we should not trust in ourselves but in God who raises the dead" (2Corinthians 1:8-9). So think then, what is the meaning of the 'sentence of death'?

Paul had reached a level of depression that stopped him from working, and the only one who was able to work was God, who created life from death.

So if Paul had a simple illness he might have sought healing in medicine, if he had any problem on earth he might have sought a solution from his own wise mind or from his advisers, but he had reached the depth of desperation; that is death, so that the resurrection was now only possible from God.

Have you ever realised that only God can solve all your problems, even if you are at the point of death? Have you ever realised how wonderful it is for God to change your condition from weakness to strength, and from death to life?

Our own Orthodox Christian faith is a continuation of Abraham's faith, as Saint Paul the apostle states "faith was accounted to Abraham for righteousness" but he didn't write for him only: "it was not just imputed to him, but also for us. It shall be imputed to us who believe in Him who raised up Jesus our Lord from the dead, who was delivered up because of our offences, and was raised because of our justification" (Romans 4:23-25)

That's why, my brother and sister, the type of faith

required from you is the faith that God can die for our sins and rise without sin, so we too die with Him for our sins and we rise with Him justified.

And now we have a cloud of witnesses from the Gospel, who light the road of our faith; because they lead by faith in Jesus Christ- the sinful woman, the gentile Canaanite woman, the foreign leper, the right hand thief… all these took Heaven by force.

Hence "We are surrounded by so great a cloud of witnesses. Let us lay aside every weight and the sin which so easily ensnares us." (Hebrews 12:1)

Faith worked in the lives of many Christians. St Paul's story is considered a great example of faith. Saul started his life persecuting the church of God, and then roamed in later years preaching the same faith to the whole world. In a similar manner, Saint Moses the Ethiopian was a chief of robbers and turned through faith into a humble saint. We cannot forget St Augustine who lived in the filthiness of sexual perversity for many years of his life, yet was transformed into a holy saint and bishop.

The Church's history is filled with saints' biographies that demonstrate how they lived the faith of Jesus' salvation. Nowadays, we follow these saints' footsteps; we taste and feel the same salvation in our own lives.

Since then, God died on the cross for our salvation,

He now stands knocking at our doors, waiting for us to live by our faith and declare our willingness to follow Him.

This brings us to the question; what if there is no evidence that God has worked in the lives of some? Why is this? It is due to the fact that this person has not approached Him in faith yet. Everyone who ever sought God in faith never failed; God does not cease to answer the consistent, faithful prayers of an individual who seeks Him honestly.

This invites us to remember Jesus' words to Jerusalem right before His crucifixion "O Jerusalem, Jerusalem, the one who kills the prophets and stones those who are sent to her! How often I wanted to gather your children together, as a hen gathers her chicks under her wings but you were not willing" (Matthew 23:37)

Surely, as a Christian, we are given great promises and a greater salvation! What then would the end of our days be if we neglect a salvation so great?! So let us step forward, trusting God with complete faith in His marvellous salvation, laying under His feet all that we want to discard, only then, will we be granted salvation. It is imperative to submit before Him all the things that we need to dispose of and not withhold things for ourselves, just as Ananias and Sapphira did, causing The Lord to withhold His salvation from us.

St Paul the apostle demonstrates to us examples of practical faith and hence gives us ways by which we can test our faith. Moreover, he lists a variety of methods; he gives us examples of Abel's obedience, Enoch who pleased The Lord through faith, and Abraham who, when called upon, faithfully obeyed The Lord. Abraham looked forward to the holy city with a glorious foundation, and gave up Isaac, believing that God will raise him from death. By faith, Moses refused to be called the son of pharaoh, considering the shame of God's people a greater fortune. Also, the faith of the Israelites, and their obedience to God led to them crossing through the sea, and destroying the walls of Jericho. Rahab the harlot was saved with her family when she believed. Many others, through faith, subdued kingdoms, worked righteousness, obtained promises, stopped the mouths of lions; others were tortured not accepting deliverance that they might obtain a better resurrection. (Hebrews 11)

All these examples, St Paul portrayed as assured pathways to experience 'liveable' faith. All these did not receive the promise, that they should not be made perfect apart from us... "Looking unto Jesus, the author and finisher of our faith" (Hebrews 11:40, 12:2)

Application:

Read chapters 11 and 12 from the book of Hebrews; note the practical advice the apostle gives about each forefather's faith and reflect on their ways to live genuinely in this faith.

Contemplate on Jesus' death for your own salvation and His resurrection for your own absolution.

CHAPTER TWO
Freedom in the Way

The Christian concept of freedom.

"For you brethren, have been called to liberty, only do not use liberty as an opportunity for the flesh, but through love serve one another" (Galatians 5:13).

The cross as a pathway to freedom.

"I have been crucified with Christ, it is no longer I who live in the flesh, I live by faith in the son of God who loved me and gave Himself for me" (Galatians 2:20)

Christ's name has been called upon many, a significant number of Christians attend church regularly and partake of the sacraments; yet, they are still slaves to the world. "For to be carnally minded is death…because the carnal mind is enmity against God." (Romans 8:6-7)

Being released from this world's possessions, desires, busyness and worries is an essential part of the soul's brilliance and its connection with God.

In the book titled "The life of prayer", our soul (whose

source is God) is likened to a bird longing to soar through the sky of prayer; yet is bound by numerous strings to the earth. Each time it attempts to take off, it falls again until its wings break and it gets exhausted. Before flight is possible, these strings must be cut.

The carnal mind is enmity against God.

Please do not misunderstand. God does not imply that we should neglect our bodily needs. As a matter of fact, the body's comfort is an essential component to the soul's recuperation. In other words, we will not be able to worship God without the flesh in this life. Having said that, there is a difference between obsession and care. A young man can spend hours in front of the mirror obsessed by his looks, while another may use the mirror to check he is presentable, not overly concerned by his attire or hair, as long as it looks respectable.

The same concept applies to food, there are so many people living solely to satisfy their appetites while others are content with basic meals. The whole world, with all its contents, should be seen as a means not an end. Nothing should enslave our thinking or attention. Many have been called to live with The Lord, yet, they intentionally became enslaved to this world's possessions, not wanting to free themselves from it.

We have heard many stories of people who became

slaves to their fortunes and focussed on money, which became their distraction from God. In regards to this, St Paul reminds us to be as "those who use this world as not misusing it. For the form of this world is passing away." (1Corinthians: 7:31).

Have you not noticed my friend, that many people claim that they worship God but are in fact slaves to the world and to the body?

Freedom in Christianity

Various concepts of freedom have been discussed by many. Every leader, disciple, and even Jesus Himself spoke about freedom, however; only Christianity has given freedom its true meaning.

Some freedom concepts involve freedom from slavery or the freedom from society's restraints. Some think that freedom is to break free and unleash every physical and intellectual desire the person might have; but whoever has experienced this type of freedom has confirmed that it is a road to misery.

The scientists who study ethics suggest that freedom is exercising your right without interfering with the right of others. From this perspective, they preserve the individual's social right, but they disregard the true meaning of freedom. Thereby, the individual is denied his happiness and freedom for the sake of the false definition of freedom.

Deviants from Christian principles advocate an extremely dangerous concept of freedom, which is to be free of any religious practice of the church; ie from all the fasting, prayers and rituals. They propose that believing in Jesus is sufficient alone to live a Christian life!

Those who recommend that religion should be free from all doctrine are simply choosing an easier path that doesn't get to heaven. "Because narrow is the gate and difficult is the way that leads to life and there are few who find it" (Matthew 7:14)

Using the same false concept of freedom, satan sought to deceive even Jesus when He fasted and said to him "If you are the son of God command that these stones become bread" (Matthew 4:3). Jesus refused satan's proposal, staying the course of the 'narrow gate'.

This is what satan tempts many of these deviants with, saying, come and I will show you an easier way. Even today, satan uses the same technique repeatedly: why not take the easier way? However, if we ponder this, we will find that the true freedom of Christianity is to free oneself from any sinful desires and lusts of the flesh. Freedom in Christianity is the release of the spirit in order to achieve liberty from darkness. The concept of freedom in Christianity is driven by abundant love to God and others without being controlled by the flesh.

It is the freedom of the sons and daughters of God "Therefore, if the Son makes you free, you shall be free indeed"(John 8:36). It is liberty to love God with all one's heart and might, without restraint or confinement.

St Peter described those who did not comprehend the meaning of freedom as people who, although they 'promise them liberty, they themselves are slaves of corruption, for by whom a person is overcome, by him also he is brought into bondage.' (2Peter 2:19). The person who can love others even though that other is the enemy, is he who knows how to apply the words of St. Paul "I Discipline my body and bring it into subjection, lest when I have preached to others, I myself should become disqualified" (1 Corinthians 9:27). It is this person who knows how to nurture his body as a gift from God to serve God.

In the past, some deluded extremists, thinking even the church's rites impinge on their freedom, called for the banning of the church rites, including the ceasing of the offering of the body and blood of our saviour in the Holy Communion! This misguided pursuit of false freedom made them lose Christ Himself!

Luckily, our church is wise. In order to ensure the benefit of every believer, the church's rites including prayers, fasting, and worshipping are designed for all Christians to follow, not only apostles and saints. These rites act as a guard and a guide on our way to heaven; in return, everyone will be granted grace and blessings according to his/her capabilities, to live in freedom. Not the freedom of the body but the freedom of the soul.

St Paul invited us to contemplate the true meaning of freedom; he invited us to consider the positive side of it; which is the delicious fruit of release from sin and its union with God.

"All things are lawful for me but not all things are helpful. All things are lawful for me but not all things edify. Let no one seek his own but each one the other's well being" (1Corinthians 10:23-24)

"Therefore, if food makes my brother stumble, I will never again eat meat, lest I make my brother stumble." (1 Corinthians 8:13)

And thus, setting myself free from food and drink is not only for the freedom of my own soul, but also to avoid making my brother stumble, and for the sake of my brother's salvation, for whom Christ died.

And in this states St James "Therefore, to him who knows to do good and does not do it, to him it is sin" (James 4:17). Thus James the Apostle urges us to the highest levels of self; to live not for ourselves but for others.

"Let this mind be in you which was also in Christ Jesus, who, being in the form of God, did not consider it robbery to be equal with God, but made Himself of no reputation, taking the form of a bondservant, and coming in the likeness of men - Let each of you look out not only for his own interests, but also for the interests of others." (Philippians 2:4)

Christianity rejects the introverted self; it instead offers the highest form of freedom to everyone. It contains people like Anthony the Hermit, who fled from all people, then travelled promptly to Alexandria to help Athanasius in his defence of the Orthodox Church.

Thus, was Jesus Christ's ministry on earth. All day, He did good to everyone He met, freely. Even to those who crucified him, He asked that God would forgive their sins. So also did Stephen, as his master-Jesus- did, asked God not to charge the people who stoned him with that sin - and so did all the servants of the early church, dedicating themselves to walk Christ's path until death for the salvation of themselves and others. Hence, no man lives for himself alone but for others.

Application:

Sit alone and confront yourself with all the earthly attachments that are taking your freedom from you, and bring them to Jesus to set you free.

The Cross; a Way to Freedom

"Whoever wants to be My disciple, let him deny himself and bear his cross and follow me". The cross with its pains and sorrows is compulsory to reach Christ for the Christian; on the other hand the Cross is a heavy load for those who are not yet set free by Christ. The cross is not only a light weight but also a desire for those who are freed by Christ, and that's why the saints freely and willingly sought it.

At a time in Egypt, the magistrate "Alhakim bi'amrallah" ordered that every Christian should carry a cross in public at all times weighing five pounds. This was designed to humiliate the Christians publicly. Some Christians carried it with much grumbling and anger. They found it a very heavy burden. One night the magistrate passed by a house while disguised and heard a strange and rhythmic 'clacking' sound. Curios, he peeped through the key hole of the house and saw a Christian working on a loom, and at the same time carrying his cross, when he didn't need to in private! Whenever the loom moved, the cross moved on his neck. Such was his fondness for the cross, he saw this as an opportunity to literally carry his cross, even when he wasn't compelled to do so by law.

So, whenever a person puts his sins and lust behind him he will be able to carry the cross not on his back, but rather, in his heart. Everyone thought that poor man working on the loom must have been depressed but the truth was he was full of joy.

The strangest thing to understand that pertains to Jesus Christ is the cross. Yet it is a non-negotiable condition of Christianity. While other religions might promise ease, or a materialistic life of abundance or rest, Jesus Himself reminds us "In the world, you will have tribulation" (John 16:33) "Strive to enter through the narrow gate" (Luke 13:24).

Despite this seemingly difficult, even paradoxical offering, the message of Jesus Christ has been spread without spear, sword or violence…how marvellous!

God revealed the truth behind the world to us, in order that we should take a stand apart from it. So that we should leave the world willingly for our love of Christ. When we walk with him, we receive abundant grace, peace and joy. Often the Christian who cultivates the virtues described by Christ in his life is valued and successful in his career and family life.

All earthly and materialistic gifts are given to all people weather evil or good and indeed to all animals by God as a practical demonstration of His love to the world. God gave all things life and knows what is needed for our life. He has never delayed to give us physical sustenance. This is because this level of materialistic life is the basest, most simple level of humanity. Jesus reminds us to 'Seek first the kingdom of God and His righteousness and all these things shall be added to you' (Matthew 6:33).

The life in Christianity is the Way of the cross, having said that, it is not of a burden nor is it painful, even if others describe it this way.

Contemplate my dear brethren on the cross of Jesus… while He was suffering an enormous physical pain, St Paul states; 'who for the joy that was set before Him endured the cross, despising the shame' (Hebrews 12:2).

There in the depths of a Philippian jail, one can imagine St Paul empathizing with Christ on the cross, almost as two similar prisoners, both beaten badly, both with their legs immobilized; one locked in the stocks, the other nailed to the wood.

What then, in this painful contemplation of Christ's suffering on the cross was Paul and his companions led to do? One would expect terror, moaning, tears, perhaps despair. Indeed the conditions within a prison are designed to cause these exact emotions.

However despite their discomfort and pain, these prisoners did the unexpected:- they rose up to chant praises and pray at midnight! All the other prisoners woke to see this marvellous and confusing scene. Was it possible for the body to be racked with pain but the soul to be at peace and indeed rejoicing?

Furthermore, could the cross, laid upon the body became the source of joy in the soul? Paul's spirit was so wonderful and attractive that the other prisoners believed in God at that moment.

In the Gospel of Luke, it was recorded that the disciples were brought to a place in which they were beaten and threatened not to talk about Jesus Christ in any place. Upon their release, they rejoiced and praised because they were worthy to suffer for His name. Did it stop their preaching? No. Moreover, it encouraged them, to increase their efforts in preaching His name!

The willingness of a person to carry the cross comes from the correction of the superficial, simplistic view that the cross is only suffering, to the internal mystery that the cross is joy.

So say 'hello' and 'welcome' to the cross. If the cross is necessary to carry, then we should carry it because it completes our life and we are content to share a portion of Christ's experience.

Saints have challenged the pain of carrying the cross. Despite the torture and suffering, they remained insistent to be called by the Lord's name. St Paul's letter to the Hebrews reminds us that 'They were stoned, they were sawn asunder, were tempted, were slain with the sword; they wandered about in sheepskins and goatskins; being destitute, afflicted, tormented; of whom the world was not worthy: they wandered in deserts; and in mountains, and in dens and caves of the earth.' (Hebrews 11:37-38)

The amazing thing about these saints who demanded the presence of the cross in their lives, is that when they found no outward cross in their lives, they entered their 'inner room' and carried the internal cross that was in their souls and hearts . You see, when a man doesn't face external challenges, he sits alone and begins turning inwardly, searching himself for his errors, praying to God and thus in this manner, begins to carry his inner cross.

Application

If you haven't carried the cross yet, sit by yourself, gather all your mistakes and problems and lay them at the foot of the cross. Now all you must do is pray and ask for God's forgiveness. God will make these heavy problems lighter.

CHAPTER THREE
Sacred Love in The Way

"Then one of the Pharisees asked Him to eat with him. And He went to the Pharisee's house, and sat down to eat. And behold, a woman in the city who was a sinner, when she knew that *Jesus* sat at the table in the Pharisee's house, brought an alabaster flask of fragrant oil, and stood at His feet behind *Him* weeping; and she began to wash His feet with her tears, and wiped *them* with the hair of her head; and she kissed His feet and anointed *them* with the fragrant oil. Now when the Pharisee who had invited Him saw *this,* he spoke to himself, saying, "This Man, if He were a prophet, would know who and what manner of woman *this is* who is touching Him, for she is a sinner." And Jesus answered and said to him, "Simon, I have something to say to you." So he said, "Teacher, say it." "There was a certain creditor who had two debtors. One owed five hundred denarii, and the other fifty. And when they had nothing with which to repay, he freely forgave them both. Tell Me, therefore, which of them will love him more?" Simon answered and said, "I suppose the *one* whom he forgave more." And He said to him, "You have rightly judged." Then He turned to the woman and said to Simon, "Do you see this woman? I entered your house; you gave Me no water for My feet, but she has washed My feet with her tears and wiped *them* with the hair of her head. You gave Me no kiss, but this woman has not ceased to kiss My feet since the time I came in. You did not anoint My head with oil, but this woman has anointed My feet with fragrant oil.

Therefore I say to you, her sins, which *are* many, are forgiven, for she loved much. But to whom little is forgiven, *the same* loves little."

Then He said to her, "Your sins are forgiven." (Luke 7:36-48)

+++

The scale of love in worship is summarised in Jesus' words: "Her sins which are many are forgiven for she loved much. But to whom little is forgiven, the same loves little" (Luke 7:47)

The way to love God is through thanksgiving: "Oh give thanks to the Lord, for He is good and His mercy endures forever" (Psalm 136:1). Another way is through contemplating the cross: "But God demonstrates his own love towards us in that while we were still sinners, Christ died for us." (Romans 5:8)

The Way to Christ is easy. The simple person finds it.

Sacred Love in The Way

It was the way taken by the sinful woman... It is the way of sacred love. 'Because she loved much,' her many sins were forgiven. The Pharisee who invited Jesus, objected and doubted the divinity of Christ, he spoke to himself saying, "This man if he were a prophet, would know who and what manner of woman this is who is touching Him, for she is a sinner."

In a similar incident, Judas Iscariot objected when Mary the sister of Lazarus did similarly, asking, "Why was the fragrant oil not sold for three hundred denarii and given to the poor?" (John 12:5) .... God looks to a person's intent, not the quantity.

The Lord praised and blessed the woman who offered all she had in the two coins-which were of almost no value. Moreover, He commanded that the story of this woman be mentioned wherever the gospel is preached.

Let us ponder on this together, when the sinful woman and the widow with the two coins are compared to the disciples at the time of Jesus' final days, which of them knew Christ and knew the way?

Clearly 'She who loved much' perceived Jesus as her saviour, while the disciples had not yet understood that he was their saviour.

Jesus wanted to give us a practical lesson in "Quality

versus Quantity" from the story of the widow who put her two coins into the offertory.

Our numerous fasts, prayers, readings and charity will count for nothing in the last day, otherwise the Pharisees and the Scribes would be far ahead of us all. We will be astonished when we find that those who have superseded us are the likes of the sinful woman and, the poor who gave out of their own need, who we once thought we would be ahead of in Heaven because we gave them charity!

Similarly, the illiterate and those who never read the Holy Bible like we have, but merely believed that the Lord Jesus died for their salvation and resurrected to make them righteous, will beat us to the eternal goal.

Did all of these people strive to reach Christ as much as us? Have they struggled and studied as we did? Perhaps not. However their simple hearts were filled with tremendous love for Christ. Such is the measure of God. Intent, rather than means, quality over quantity.

We must remember then, that whatever we do, even if it is good in nature, if it is devoid of love and passion for Christ, it is a waste. Additionally, no matter how useful it is to others it is useless to us, "For what will it profit a man if he gains the whole world, and loses his own soul?" (Mark 8:36)

Firstly- Prayer

Prayer is simply an expression of our feelings and needs towards God, a communication with God. Prayer is not only uni-directional: from us to God, but it is for the benefit of us and our relationship with God. Whoever prays in order to cross a task off their daily list, remains on the first rungs of the ascent to Heaven and needs to remember that it is not God who needs prayer so much as we ourselves.

Then what are the motives of prayer?

Prayer is the expression of a deeply embedded longing within our souls to speak to God. It is the private and personal discussion between a bride and groom. It not only pleases the groom to hear the bride's voice, but moreover he longs for and cherishes her voice.

God reminds us in the book of Revelation, "behold I stand at the door and knock…." (Revelation 3:20) the decision to open the door is in your hands.

Additionally, prayer is like a conversation between a son and his father, full of longing and deep love. It is with these feelings that we should approach God in prayer.

Then tell me, why is it that sometimes I pray a lot, but do not receive what I ask?

How many times have you attended the divine liturgy and taken nothing from it? Why is that the case?

This situation warrants a review of one's self, and it is the wise person who conducts such an audit promptly once alerted to the issue. Ask yourself, what were my feelings when I attended the liturgy? Was my heart full of longing and love for Christ? Was this feeling real and practical in action? Ie. Did it drive me to wake up early, prepare myself from the night before etc.? Was I impatient for that hour? Did I pray to God to fill me and satisfy my needs?

When I arrived at Church, did I thank God, expressing my love for Him through a prayer or calm worship eg. lighting a candle in front of a saint's icon?

Did I stand during Holy liturgy conversing with God, privately, feeling overwhelmed when contemplating how much God does for me?

Moreover, when I lifted up my eyes and saw the crucified Jesus on top of the altar, did this remind me of His great love for me? Did I imagine myself living with the Lord, his angels and his saints in Heaven? Did I remember that I am being personally invited to partake of His Holy Feast to become one in Jesus Christ? In short did I 'live' the Holy Liturgy?

Or instead, did I wake up tired and lazy, arrive late to the liturgy, stand bored and distracted thinking of what I will do when this is over? Then why do I wonder why I ultimately gain nothing? Did I see the Holy Liturgy as an inconvenience?

Furthermore, what is it that motivates me in my individual prayer?

Is it love and longing for a private talk with Jesus, thanking God through a sigh…or a tear…or prostrations… or simple words…or by asking Him about the mysteries of His kingdom…or about the virtues and qualities I desire for my spiritual life? Do I ask with insistence, humility and love?

Do I feel thankful to Christ my God at every moment, recalling his love periodically and thus transforming my life into one continuous prayer? One helpful way to focus the mind is to repeat phrases like: 'But I give myself to prayer', 'Thank you my Lord Jesus Christ', 'Have mercy on me my Lord Jesus Christ', 'Help me, my Lord Jesus Christ' and 'I glorify you my Lord Jesus Christ'.

In this manner you may enter the path, my beloved, and approach Jesus to present to Him your heart, tears, love and yearning for Him, just as the sinful woman did.

In return, He will look at you in a beautiful and meek way, full of love and sincerity, and He will grant you all that you need and more; even if your sins were greater than those of the sinful woman.

One of the mysteries of deep prayer is the disconnection of time from reality. The stories of the saints regularly describe situations where saints lost all reckoning of time during deep prayer, as if consumed, by the sacred love of Jesus, their minds 'detached' from time. It is recorded about St Arsanios that he had so developed a prayer discipline, that he would become 'absorbed in prayer' - beginning prayer at sunset and continuing throughout the night, until the sun rose again and shone into his face, startling him from his reverie.

Secondly: Reading of the Holy Book

If prayer is an expression of a deeply embedded longing within our souls to speak to God, then the study of the Holy Bible is the desire to hear God's voice.

When Jesus went to Lazarus' house and spoke about the Kingdom of Heaven, Mary, Lazarus' sister delighted in listening to it. Her sister, Martha however, criticised her for neglecting to help her with the household chores and instead sitting and listening to Jesus.

Mary's longing and love for Jesus drove her to put

aside her chores and instead sit at His feet and listen. Thus, she sought the good, everlasting share. In a similar manner, the sinful woman reached the Lord Christ. Being a woman of ill-repute, she ought to have avoided being seen by such a large crowd due to their inevitable, judgemental stares and hurtful remarks. Remarkably, she pushes all of this behind her and approaches Christ with a boldness, born of repentance and love, baring her vulnerability before Jesus:- and for her efforts- she hears the sweetest, most comforting words a sinner can imagine from Christ: "Your sins are forgiven".

The stories of the sinful woman and Mary Lazarus' sister aren't recorded in the Gospels for their sakes alone, but also for ours. They give us a type of 'character role' to help us live vicariously through these women in these situations and experience their emotions in order to draw closer to Jesus and receive from Him what they received. So that our hearts might increasingly desire to listen to His life-giving words.

As a person might long tirelessly to listen to a loved ones' words, how much more then, should one long for the words of The One who loves us and died for us?

Let us review the ways we listen to Jesus' voice and read His Holy Book.

How do I approach reading the Bible? Is it to increase my knowledge and understanding of Jesus

Christ? Is there pride mingled in my reading? I mean; Am I proud of my knowledge of the Bible or my ability to read it?

Do I read it to prepare a good Sunday School lesson, or do I read it out of habit? Has it become a task to read a chapter every day?

While these are all good objectives, what have I benefited from them in my life and in my relationship with Jesus?

Surely I should read with passion and love, the words of my 'Beloved'.

Psalm 119 is a great example of David's longing to hear God's words when he writes:

20 "My soul breaks with longing

For Your judgements at all times."

24 "Your testimonies also *are* my delight

And my counsellors."

47 "And I will delight myself in Your commandments,

Which I love."

72 "The law of Your mouth *is* better to me

Than thousands of *coins of* gold and silver."

162 "I rejoice at Your word

As one who finds great treasure."

Hence, I must ask myself: Am I motivated by longing and love for Jesus to read His words? If the honest answer is 'yes', then I can be sure I am on the right track toward Heaven, and if 'no' then I must seek to remedy this, if indeed Heaven is my goal.

Gauge your 'spiritual temperature' using your attitude toward reading God's words as your 'spiritual thermometer' are you hot or lukewarm?!!!

The Book of Acts teaches us that "It is more blessed to give than to receive" (Acts: 20:35). What an unusual idea that seems logically backward! For example, in this earthly life, the basic premise of business is to sell goods or services at a profit. A wise merchant or vendor gives a little but gains more from a customer. How then can the Christian idea make sense that the one spending gains blessing above the one receiving?

My friend, this verse reveals a Christian mystery. As a matter of fact, the giver's blessing is multiplied here on earth and in Heaven. Herein lies the mystery. The condition when giving to unlock blessings is to give as if I am giving to Christ Himself. Only then, will He give me abundantly in return. Christ will never be pleased if I follow His Way only for personal, financial or materialistic gain. My giving should be based on my love to The Lord.

In his attempts to keep you from attaining virtues, satan often uses a 'stepped' approach. It is no different with charity:

First he will try to convince you not to give. This manifests in sudden thoughts like 'We are in uncertain financial times', 'Who knows what might happen tomorrow?', 'I already give to other causes' and 'I am better off using this money for…'.

If you won't be dissuaded and insist on giving, he will employ his second phase attack: Robbery. He will try to rob you of your heavenly reward by convincing you that what you are doing needs to be announced publicly or at least told to others. This will often manifest in thoughts like: 'this is a great public good, others should know about it!', 'You are a great example to others!' and 'Others will look up to you and donate too!'.

If you won't be robbed and insist on giving in secret, then he launches his third phase attack: Pride. Beware of thoughts that suddenly assail your mind, like: 'I am better than others who didn't give' or 'Nobody else gave like I did!'.

In order to survive satan's attacks I must see charity as something done for the sake of my love to the Lord, as in the case of giving to the poor. "Assuredly, I say to you, in as much as you did it to one of the least of these My brethren you did it to Me" (Matthew: 25:40). Hence, I will love and appreciate the poor as brothers of Christ; only then will my heart enlarge and fill with love; and the more I love others, the more my heart will draw closer to God.

The following story is an assurance of this concept of love for others.

A shoemaker woke up from his sleep on a very cold night after he dreamt that he will meet Jesus that day. He cooked delicious meals and prepared warm soup in case Jesus would be seeking warmth and waited eagerly for His visit. After waiting for an extended period of time, he looked from the window into the darkness, only to find someone sitting outside in the cold, covering his face and holding a staff.

The shoemaker rushed out to him thinking it was Jesus. As he drew closer to greet him, he realised that it was just an old man. Nonetheless, the shoemaker rushed him inside and gave him a hot drink and some food. As he watched him eat, he noted that he was shivering from the cold, so he gave him his own coat to wear. Satisfied, the old man left after a few hours, and the shoe-maker sat back down to wait for Jesus. Every time he looked from the window there was no one else on the street, so the shoemaker thought, he could pass the time by reading the Bible. He opened the book and his eyes fell upon the passage: "then they will answer Him saying, 'Lord, when did we see you hungry or thirsty or a stranger or naked or sick or in prison and did not minister to you?' Then He will answer them 'Assuredly I say to you in as much as you did it to one of the least of these my brethren you did it to me' (Matthew: 25-40). The shoemaker, suddenly understanding, closed the bible and stood to pray, thanking Jesus for His visit and for giving him the blessing of serving one of His brothers.

Do you see now how giving, benefits the giver? Lets see who else can benefit from the act of giving.

Let us revisit the story of the sinful woman who brought an alabaster flask of fragrant oil to anoint Jesus. Judas objected, and asked why this oil wasn't sold and its proceeds spent on the poor? What a corrupt view of giving! It is not for the poor's benefit that we give; it is for our own sakes. Christ is capable of giving the poor and satisfying them without us. All that God requires is our hearts filled with compassion and love. That is why God loved the widow who gave her two mites. What could two mites do? They couldn't satisfy any need; but Jesus blessed her because He saw her heart filled with love for God.

Therefore my brethren, we should weigh our

donations against the love in our hearts. This is why the church includes in the oblation of the offertory those who brought gifts, as well as those wished to give but couldn't; they are both equally blessed by God, because God looks into the heart, to see a person's intent.

The following story illustrates how a person can draw blessings from God. One day, a severe famine occurred in a particular country due to a prolonged drought. One of the monks had only three loaves of bread left. His plan was to eat them slowly over time because he was unsure what would happen afterwards. As he was carefully storing the bread, a stranger passed by his cell, asking for food, so the monk gave him the first loaf of bread. Soon afterwards, a second then a third stranger knocked on his door requesting food and the monk couldn't keep himself from giving them the other loaves of bread because of the love in his heart for others in need. He followed Christ's path as St Paul said "For you know the grace of our Lord Jesus Christ that though He was rich, yet for your sakes He became poor that you through His poverty might become rich." (2Corinthians 8:9). God saw from above, and couldn't withhold the rain any longer due to the love of this monk.

The service

When we discuss abundant giving, we don't only mean the materialistic donations, there is the giving of time, effort, pride and obedience.

The service nowadays surely differs from the service at the time of the first church. There are many servants and each of them has their own view about the service. Someone could give from his time for the sake of showing off, or for being glorified by others. Another person might serve so he/she can fill their leisure time and once he/she becomes occupied, leaves the service. Another might be spending the effort for no apparent valuable objective.

There is only one acceptable service; the service of the person that loves Christ from all his/her heart because he/she has tasted His great salvation; and his/her heart was filled by the love of Jesus Christ. The servant's heart that overflows with love, strives to help others and seek their salvations too. Therefore, if Christ Himself is not the cornerstone of our giving, and then our effort and service will fade and die.

Let us ask ourselves, why do our services today seem spiritless and hollow? As if we are just 'going through the motions'? It is because our love for others has grown cold. Our tears, heartache and prayers for those away from the church-the body of Christ- has ceased; our service and good deeds have turned into a parody or materialistic habit. Even our preparation of a Sunday School lesson has become purely educational without any spirituality, even if it is evident that the souls we are serving are drifting away from Jesus.

The measures of success in the service have changed from seeking those away from Christ to the number of servants who attend, and how many children were in class today. In this way, our service has become rigid, cold and meaningless, unconcerned for the salvation of others.

Jesus served differently, in complete love and gentleness, He walked long hours in the heat of the day, so He could save the Samaritan women. He blessed the sinful woman who perfumed his head, and did not concern Himself with the great man that invited Him to his feast. He declared how heaven rejoices over one repentant sinner more than ninety nine others who don't need repentance.

Jesus didn't give attention to the appearance nor to the numbers of people. He rejoiced when he found the lost coin and the lost sheep; even more, He hugged His prodigal son when he returned home.

In the same manner, my dear brethren, if you would like to offer an acceptable service, then you are invited to measure your service according to Jesus; while we were yet sinners, Jesus revealed His love to us. We must have hearts full of love towards the salvation of others. St Paul called upon us to do this "That in every way, whether in pretense or in truth, Christ is preached; and in this rejoice, yes and I will rejoice" (Philippians: 1:18)

St Paul knew the essence of a good service, explaining its value in his eternal words "Just as it is right for me to think this of you all, because I have you in my heart, inasmuch as both in my chains and in the defence and confirmation of the gospel, you all are partakers with me of grace." (Philippians: 1:7).

Even in his final letter to the church in Ephesus. "And when they had come to Him, he said to them: "You know, from the first day that I came to Asia, in what manner I always lived among you, serving the Lord with all humility, with many tears and trials which happened to me by the plotting of the Jews; how I kept back nothing that was helpful, but proclaimed it to you, and taught you publicly and from house to house, testifying to Jews and also to Greeks, repentance toward God and faith toward our Lord Jesus Christ. And see, now I go bound in the spirit to Jerusalem, not knowing the things that will happen to me there, except that the Holy Spirit testifies in every city, saying that chains and tribulations await me. But none of these things move me; nor do I count my life dear to myself, so that I may finish my race with joy, and the ministry which I received from the Lord Jesus, to testify to the gospel of the grace of the God.

"And indeed, now I know that you all, among whom I have gone preaching the kingdom of God, will see my face no more. Therefore I testify to you this day that I am innocent of the blood of all men. For I have not shunned to declare to you the whole counsel of God. Therefore take heed to yourselves and to all the flock, among which the Holy Spirit has made you overseers, to shepherd the church of God which He purchased with His own blood. For I know this, that after my departure savage wolves will come in among you, not sparing the flock. Also from among yourselves men will rise up, speaking perverse things, to draw away the disciples after themselves. Therefore watch, and remember that for three years I did not cease to warn everyone night and day with tears" (Acts 20:18-31)

The service of sacred love and the service of salvation is also a service of kneeling prayers.

+++

Our Relationship with Others

A certain lawyer asked Jesus saying, what shall I do to inherit eternal life? Then the lawyer said, you shall love the Lord your God with all your heart, with all your soul, with all your strength, and with all your mind, and your neighbour as yourself. And Jesus said to him, you have answered rightly…do this and you will live.

"And who is my neighbour?" asked the lawyer.

Jesus answered by telling the story of the Good Samaritan, and how a stranger acted mercifully toward a Jew, traditionally an enemy to him. Conversely, his neighbours and fellow Jews (The priest and the Levite) didn't help him but left him dying on the road...then Jesus said to him...go and do likewise.

Hence, our relationship with others must be built on love, even for our enemies. But can this be done? How can we love our enemies? Certainly, in one way it is a very difficult thing to do ...yet, in another it is quite easy. Difficult, if we think by human standards, yet easy by divine standards.

Cain killed his own brother, Abel, in the very early beginnings of humanity, while the only begotten Son, Jesus, died for the sinners when He was without sin.

While the love commandment seems heavy to bear in the eyes of the world, it is easy for true Christians, because the person who cannot love others must not have experienced the divine love of God.

Only the heart of a person who has loved God, become satisfied by Him (because He is the fountain of love) and become one with Him can overflow with love towards others. He or she has become united with the God of love...how could one possibly not love others then?

"Beloved, let us love one another, for love is of God; and everyone who loves is born of God and knows God" (1 John 4:7)

"God is love, and he who abides in love abides in God, and God in him" (1 John 4:16)

Whoever believes that Jesus is the Christ is born of God... For this is the love of God, that we keep His commandments. And His commandments are not burdensome. For whatever is born of God overcomes the world. And this is the victory that has overcome the world—our faith. Who is he who overcomes the world, but he who believes that Jesus is the Son of God? (1 John 5:1-5)

'For God so loved the world that He gave His only begotten Son, that whoever believes in Him should not perish but have everlasting life" (John 3:16)

When we live with God and follow His commandments, we become united with Him and become His children, in His image.

Consequently, our love toward others becomes easy-second nature. It even becomes natural because God is dwelling within us, such that we love increasingly without effort and also without asking for anything in return.

This love is complete because it originates not from us but from God who is living within us.

If you are finding the godly commandment-to love everyone- difficult, then dig into your relationship with God first and investigate how connected you are with Him. Is He united with you? Examine this closely so you don't lose your way, because he who hates his brother is a murderer…

We have to stop and reflect along the way asking: Why is God not listening to our prayers? Why doesn't He give us when we ask? Why doesn't He accept our fasts?

My brethren, if the way to God is the love of Christ, and if everything in our lives and worship is an expression of loving Christ, then how do we get there ?...

First: The life of Thanksgiving

When you contemplate on a little child and the way the child develops feelings of love towards his father, we realise that the child looks up to his parents as a source of every good gift. If the child asks, his father gives, and when the father gets back home his son receives him asking: what have you brought me? Moreover, when the child gets sick he gets looked after…It's this feeling towards the father's gifts that will certainly lead to a deep loving relationship with him.

Now let's contemplate the feelings of the saints towards God. St Gregory said "You made the Earth firm for me so I can walk on it" ... Don't we all walk on Earth? But we forget it's a gift from God for us.

David the prophet walks in the midst of the green pastures, in front of him are his sheep. This made him realise that God watches over him like these sheep, so he sang: "The Lord is my shepherd; I shall not want".

This exercise is not hard, in fact it's quite easy. You have to thank God every time He grants you a gift. Thank Him when you wake up in the morning for granting you life. Your first words in the morning should be "Thank you God for You have given me a safe and peaceful night".

Moreover, when you eat, thank Him for His bounties. During your working day you can still connect with God without anyone noticing, thanking Him for the success He grants you at work…similarly in all aspects of your material life.

But there is a greater aspect to thank God for, which is to thank Him for all that He has given you in your spiritual life.

The last prayer, at the end of the liturgy is "And let us also thank God the Father, for He has made us worthy to stand in this holy place and lift up our hands.."

When God gives you spiritual contemplations during your reading of the Bible, thank Him. Thank Him when you grow in any sacred virtue, for He is the source of every good gift.

Remember the words of St Isaac the Syrian "there is no gift which is not multiplied by blessing except that which is without thanksgiving"

Consequently, the Church organised the thanksgiving prayer at the beginning of every communal or individual prayer.

The thanksgiving prayer is an honest expression of our love toward God.

Such a relationship between the father and his son is one of thanksgiving and acknowledgement of God's grace.

Thanksgiving is the greatest way to strengthen our love towards God. St Paul reached the ultimate depth in sensing God's gifts when he said "For in Him we live, and move, and have our being." (Acts 17:28)

Second: Jesus on The Cross

The greatest event that shapes our lives and affects us is the death of Jesus, for our salvation. St Paul says "For when we were still without strength, in due time Christ died for the ungodly. For scarcely for a righteous man will one die; yet perhaps for a good man someone would even dare to die. But God demonstrates His own love toward us, in that while we were still sinners, Christ died for us." (Romans 5:6-8)

We were condemned to eternal death because of our sins, then a man stepped forward and died for us so we could live.

His love that he loved us with, obliges us to love Him from all the heart, mind and strength.

For this reason, the Church has placed the icon of Christ hanging on the cross on top of the altar, before us all the time. It is the greatest matter our minds must rise to. Our feelings when we pray should echo St Paul's: "For I decided to know nothing among you except Jesus Christ and Him crucified." (1Corinthians 2:2)

A short story on this: A saint had a disciple whom he visited one day. He found an amazing thing in his disciple's Bible: every page had the word "Jesus" blotted out or smudged. He asked his disciple about this, who, at first, remained silent. After the saint insisted, his disciple answered: When I read His name, tears pour forth from my eyes as I remember His salvation and death for me on the cross. My tears fall upon His name.

Jesus' crucifixion must be our contemplation every day, as proof of our love to God for His love to us.

This should be my ultimate goal: to be saved by Jesus' death for me and to love Him with all my heart, because of the love that He flooded me with, when I was unworthy.

Applications:

1. Practice the habit of thanking Jesus for His gifts.
2. Always contemplate what Jesus did on the cross for you.

CHAPTER FOUR
I Am the Way

+ "I am the **way**, the truth, and the life. No one comes to the Father except through me" (John 14:6)

+ "He who has seen Me has seen the Father…I *am* in the Father and the Father in Me." (John 14:9-10)

"I go to prepare a place for you. And if I go and prepare a place for you, I will come again and receive you to Myself; that where I am, *there* you may be also. And where I go you know, and the way you know."

Thomas said to Him, "Lord, we do not know where You are going, and how can we know the way?"

Jesus said to him, "I am the **way**, the truth, and the life. No one comes to the Father except through Me." (John 14:2-6)

Thus, Jesus made it clear for us that He is the only Way to reach the Father, He wants to ensure that we know this so we do not stray from the Way, trying in vain to reach the Father through a way that is not the Son.

He who has seen me, has seen the Father

During his missionary journey through the city of Athens, St Paul noticed a shrine dedicated "to the Unknown God". How strange! We might think, however, is this not exactly what happens in all religions worldwide today? Namely that this Athenian shrine was a collective social symbol of what individuals have always done: dedicate fasts, prayers, worship and charity to 'God'; without ever knowing Him personally, but merely hearing about Him, then 'filling in the blanks' as they like! This is how every religion and indeed every human can imagine or create for themselves a God tailored to their liking.

In opposition to this 'build your own god' concept, we have in Christianity: Jesus. The Son, God incarnate, the second Godly Hypostasis, coming in a human body, and living among us on earth. St John wrote "That which was from the beginning, which we have heard, which we have seen with our eyes, which we have looked upon, and our hands have handled, concerning the Word of life" (1 John 1).

So Jesus Christ lived among us, rejoicing with those who rejoiced in the wedding at Cana of Galilee, wept when his friend Lazarus died, healed illness and felt human pain... So we can be sure He is familiar with our struggles, and every human who knows the Son is able to know the Father through Him. Humanity witnessed the love of the Father through the sacrifice of Jesus for us, we witnessed God's power in the resurrection of Lazarus from the dead. He has the power to forgive our sins, as He forgave the sins of the cripple, who then stood, collected his bed and walked. He has power over nature, as He demonstrated when He calmed the storm at sea. He has the power to fulfil all our needs, as was demonstrated at the miracles of feeding the multitudes.

Hence, we should be confident that we know the Father because we know the Son and have lived with Him. Christ Himself said that He and the Father are one. We do not pray to an 'unknown' God at all, nor an imaginary god, but the true God who demonstrated His love for us.

+++

He reconciled the heavenly with the earthly

The Way to heaven was closed to us, since Adam and Eve were ejected from the garden of Eden after they abandoned God due to their weakness. God assigned an angel to guard the Way to the tree of life, and conflict was established between God and human beings. No being was able to open that Way to heaven; no angel, no archangel, no prophet.

Opening the Way to Heaven required reconciliation between God and man, redemption of the sin committed and a death atonement on behalf of all humanity. There was no human or angel who could fulfil all these criteria, except Jesus Christ. It was only God who could break through that wall between us.

St Paul reveals to us regarding Jesus' salvific work: "having wiped out the handwriting of requirements that was against us, which was contrary to us. And He has taken it out of the Way, having nailed it to the cross" (Colossians 2:14). He was the only one who could offer redemption for our sins, and He was the only one who could open for us the Way to the Father, and hence reconcile us to the Father, as St Paul says "Now all things are of God, who has reconciled us to Himself through Jesus Christ, and has given us the ministry of reconciliation, that is, that God was in Christ reconciling the world to Himself, not imputing their trespasses to them" (2 Corinthians 5:18-19). This reconciliation was freely given, since we could not purchase it, but we were all in desperate need of it, as St Paul states "there is none righteous, no, not one" (Romans 3:11). "being justified freely by His grace through the redemption that is in Christ Jesus, whom God set forth as a propitiation by His blood, through faith, to demonstrate His righteousness, because in His forbearance God had passed over the sins that were previously committed, to demonstrate at the present time His righteousness, that He might be just and the justifier of the one who has faith in Jesus" (Romans

3:24-26). And St. Paul tells about this reconciliation in his message to the Ephesians"But now in Christ Jesus you who once were far off have been brought near by the blood of Christ. For He Himself is our peace, who has made both one, and has broken down the middle wall of separation, having abolished in His flesh the enmity, that is, the law of commandments contained in ordinances, so as to create in Himself one new man from the two, thus making peace, and that He might reconcile them both to God in one body through the cross, thereby putting to death the enmity…" (Ephesians 2:13-16)

We return now to the aforementioned question: Is it possible to reach the Father without Jesus? Is Jesus the only Way?

St. Paul writes "for if righteousness comes through the law, then Christ died in vain" (Galatians 2:21)

Everyone has committed sins, humanity was sentenced to death.

While every religions has its merits, containing varying laws and commandments, what is the value of those commandments? St. Paul says that it is such religious laws that taught him sin. "On the contrary, I would not have known sin except through the law. For I would not have known covetousness unless the law had said, "You shall not covet." But sin, taking opportunity by the commandment, produced in me all manner of evil desire. For apart from the law sin was dead. I was alive once without the law, but when the commandment came, sin revived and I died.»(Romans 7:7-9)

You can imagine the value of any religious law as a kind of mirror. A person who has some dirt on his face, looks in the mirror and sees the dirt. What he does then is up to him. Hence the mirror can help him identify the dirt on his face but can do nothing to remove it for him.

St. Paul explains that, if there were a single person who was sinless, then there wouldn't have been a need for Jesus to die, thus confirming to us that the death of Jesus is the only Way to reconcile to God.

He manifests himself in us, guiding us to the Father

For what I am doing, I do not understand. For what I will to do, that I do not practice; but what I hate, that I do. If, then, I do what I will not to do, I agree with the law that it is good. But now, it is no longer I who do it, but sin that dwells in me. For I know that in me (that is, in my flesh) nothing good dwells; for to will is present with me, but *how* to perform what is good I do not find. For the good that I will *to do,* I do not do; but the evil I will not *to do,* that I practice. Now if I do what I will not *to do,* it is no longer I who do it, but sin that dwells in me.

I Am the Way

I find then a law, that evil is present with me, the one who wills to do good. For I delight in the law of God according to the inward man. But I see another law in my members, warring against the law of my mind, and bringing me into captivity to the law of sin, which is in my members. O wretched man that I am! Who will deliver me from this body of death? (Romans 7:15-25)

We can now deduce just as St Paul the apostle did, that the reason for sin is not the law or the commandments of the law, but rather that sin emanates from the soul and the body.

The law, as good as it is, falls short of changing our nature away from sin.

Here, there must be a distinction made between Christianity and other faiths. Other faiths have had prophets and teachers with excellent commandments but what good are these commandments to me if my sin emanates from my very nature, from my own body?

In Christianity, God became incarnate in the form of man. He revealed to us a new path through Jesus Christ who took our human form. He became man. He gave us his nature and therefore we became companions in his godliness. He likened himself to us in everything.

St Paul in his epistle to the Hebrews writes "Therefore, in all things He had to be made like *His* brethren, that

He might become a merciful and faithful High Priest in things pertaining to God, to make propitiation for the sins of the people." (Hebrews 2:17)

While Christ lived on the earth, He asked "which of you convicts Me of sin?" (John 8:46). However, we are all humans with weaknesses, which of us is sinless? What we must acknowledge is that Christ was the perfect man, free from sin, 'but made Himself of no reputation, taking the form of a bondservant, and coming in the likeness of men. And being found in appearance as a man, he humbled himself and became obedient to the point of death, even the death of the cross.' (Philippians 2:7)

God abandoned what was His- glory in Heaven- and embraced what is ours- struggle and suffering on earth. It was impossible for God in his glory to be amongst us and be born of a virgin.

His glory terrorized the Israelites in the Old Testament. For this reason he abandoned his glory and became like one of us, praying to The Father like us. But for His great obedience and humility towards The Father, The Father rewarded Him with great glory. For when He spoke to The Father, He glorified Him with the glory that was His before the world was, according to Christ's own testimony in John 17:5.

Regarding glorifying the Father's name, The Father's

own voice was heard saying, "I have both glorified it and will glorify it again." (John 12:28)

Such was the way Christ lived, as an obedient Son to The Father. He was glorified as man because of His obedience. He did not sin because of the power of God within him. He revealed to us the mysterious Way back to The Father. We can now conquer sin by the power of The Father residing in us, namely the Holy Spirit. The Father is manifest in our lives through our faith and obedience.

St Paul complained about his weakness in the flesh, "Who will deliver me from this body of death?" (Romans 7:24) But in another epistle he exclaims "I can do all things through Christ who strengthens me." (Phillipians 4:13). At another instance he reveals, "when I am weak, then I am strong." (2 Corinthians 12:10).

So through our faith and union with Christ we can perform great deeds like Christ did and even greater. This is what Christ told us, but why then, don't we? The truth is, it is not we who do the great deeds but the power of Christ that abides in us. St Paul writes, "it is no longer I who live, but Christ lives in me." (Galatians 2:20). A Christian person is but a pure vessel that carries God within him.

Christ is the only Way to victory. What good are the competing ideologies of other faiths when they all fail to assist us?

The only Way forward is union with Christ.

'leaving us an example, that you should follow His steps' (1 Peter 2:21)

Our Lord Jesus lived amongst us as a perfect human. He emptied Himself, and came to the earth as the incarnate God. Each step He took was not for His sake, but for ours.

He was born in a manger, in order to teach us the first lesson: the life of humility is the beginning of the Way. It is not possible to enter the heavenly glory except through this path. In every act, and every incident in the life of Christ, you will sense the humility of the manger. He was obedient to the point of death, was baptized to fulfil all righteousness, and fasted, to teach us what an acceptable fast is. He was tempted by the devil three times, although these temptations held no power over Him. He was tempted to teach us how we should overcome temptation. The devil tempted Him with hunger, pride, and the 'easy path'. Each time, Christ prevailed by the word kept in Him. Thus, He taught us the power of the Holy Scripture in our war against the enemy.

After His victory, angels came and ministered to Him, to whom the angles minister day and night. Yet the scripture mentions the ministry of the angels to set a path before us: whoever defeats the enemy is worthy of the ministry of the angels.[1]

The Master also showed us how to treat others, how to love our enemies, and how to yearn for the salvation of all; He showed us how he saved the Samaritan woman, and how He refused to bring down fire and burn Samaria when they refused His word, despite His own disciples' urging to do so. Again, He taught us how to hate sin and love sinners, by forgiving the adulteress. He accepted hospitality and honour from tax collectors and sinners, and saved many of those whom society had discarded.

He established a path for those who wish to serve God after Him. He would spend the night in prayer, and the day doing good works and miracles. Before choosing his twelve disciples, He spent the night in prayer.

He was patient in bearing the weaknesses of His disciples, and enduring their flaws. He was humble amongst them and became their servant, demonstrating to them practical humility. He taught us how a leader should behave; washing their feet and praying for them while they slept in the garden of Gethsemane. Teaching us that the true leader serves everyone and bears other's burdens, in spite of their weakness.

He taught us how to behave in our social and civil life

---

[1] The fathers who excelled in worship – volume 2

by teaching us to give to Caesar what is Caesar's and to God what is God's. He was a loyal citizen, serving His country, obeying the leaders and fulfilling His duties.

When the time came for Him to speak the truth, He did, even if it lead to His death. His disciples taught us that 'we ought to obey God rather than men'(Acts 5:29). When the servant of the high priest struck Him, He asked 'Why do you strike me?' (John 18:23). When He saw that the temple was defiled by merchants and money changers, He was inflamed with a holy zeal, and drove them all out. Christ challenged the hypocrisy of the Pharisees and stood firm in the truth. He always valued the honesty of the soul living with God privately and intimately over the deceptive outward appearance of faith. He praised the poor widow, who gave all that she had- her whole livelihood- despite her poverty.

He was a loving and considerate person, with gentle feelings. He welcomed the children and blessed them; and He had friends whom he lodged with, such as Lazarus and his sisters. He rejoiced with those who rejoiced, and obeyed His mother when He turned the water into wine at the wedding. He wept with those who wept and consoled them, healed their sick and raised their dead.

We must walk in this life just as Christ walked, for He is the only Way which we should follow.

Lastly, follow Him to the cross; satan tempted Him

I Am the Way

to follow the easy path by saying "All these things I will give you if you will fall down and worship me" then Jesus answered: "Away with you satan, for it is written you shall worship The Lord your God and Him only you shall serve" (Matthew: 4:1-12, 13)

Jesus Christ refused to reign over the world apart from the cross. Without the cross, we wouldn't have been blessed by the holy resurrection and the continuous joy of receiving the Holy Spirit within us.

Whoever wants to follow Christ's pathway, first must be born in the manger of humility, then walk the same struggle in temptation and serving others. Let him carry his cross like Jesus did until death and rise again with Him. "This is a faithful saying, for if we died with Him, we shall also live with Him" (2Timothy2:11)

Jesus Christ is our Way, our only Way to the kingdom of heaven

He is the only access to God the Father... through Him we learned about The Father.

He reconciled heaven and earth and opened to us the doors of Heaven.

He unites with us and leads us to The Father so we can become one in Him.

He gave us a living example so we can follow in His footsteps.

Glory and honour be to our God now and forever more. Amen.

+ + + + +

Here, we ask a few reflective questions.

Q: How does Christ suffer from our inequities and shortcomings?

A: Simply because we have become one in Him. How can we commit sins while He is in us and with us. Voluntarily, Jesus carried all our sins on the cross and He was content to do so, however, He will never be satisfied with us living in sin while He is dwelling within us.

Q: How can our body parts unite with Christ?

A: St Paul asks: "Shall I then take the members of Christ and make them members of a harlot?" (1 Corinthians: 6:15). St Paul referred to the human body that Jesus Christ united with in the mystery of the Incarnation, making the bodies of all individuals a part of Christ Himself.

I Am the Way

Q: If Christ is united with us, what is our belief regarding prayer?

A: St Augustine states that He searched eagerly for Jesus everywhere he looked. In nature and in books; yet, he only found Him when he looked deeply into his own soul. This assures us that God listens to every prayer we say and responds quickly to it. As we discussed before, we will never be able to connect with God deeply unless we unleash our souls from this world's tethers.

Q: Why do we continue to sin despite being connected with Christ?

A: God doesn't impose His salvation upon us, out of respect for the individual, despite our weakness against sin, however, when we seek Him in prayers He never delays.

www.ingramcontent.com/pod-product-compliance
Lightning Source LLC
Chambersburg PA
CBHW031203160426
43193CB00008B/481